THE ULTIMATE

Volcanoes

BOOK FOR KIDS

BELLANOVA

MELBOURNE · SOFIA · BERLIN

Volcanoes: The Ultimate Volcano Book

Visit us at www.bellanovabooks.com

Imprint: Bellanova Books

CONTENTS

WELCOME TO THE
WORLD OF VOLCANOES

This is no ordinary journey, but a bold adventure into the heart of our living planet. You're about to uncover the fiery phenomena known as volcanoes, marvels that have molded and reshaped our Earth over millions of years.

Imagine for a moment the intense heat, the incredible power, and the magnificent beauty of a volcanic eruption. It's a sight that leaves onlookers awestruck. But rest assured, this exploration won't require heat-proof suits or gas masks! We'll be journeying through the pages of this book, where the spectacle of volcanoes can be explored from the comfort of your own home.

Starting with the basics in chapter one, we'll uncover what a volcano truly is. Far from being simple mountains with bad tempers, volcanoes are fascinating geological structures with a story to tell about the inner workings of our planet.

At the end of the book, test all your new knowledge in the volcano quiz!

So get ready to turn the page and step into a world where science, geography, history, and mythology meet - the thrilling world of volcanoes. Are you ready? Let's go!

Volcán de Fuego, Guatemala

WHAT IS A VOLCANO?

A volcano is more than just a mountain with a temper. It's a natural opening in the Earth's surface where molten rock, gases, and ash escape from deep below. This molten rock is called **magma** when it's underground, but once it reaches the surface, we call it **lava**. Don't get those two mixed up—it could be a fiery faux pas at your next volcano trivia night!

FUN FACT

There are more than 1,500 potentially active volcanoes around the world. That's a lot of molten rock!

TYPES OF VOLCANOES

Just like animals or plants, not all volcanoes are the same. There are several types, each with its own unique features and temperaments. Let's take a closer look at the differences.

Mauna Kea, Hawaii. It's so tall it gets snow annually!

Mighty Shield Volcanoes

Shield volcanoes are the gentle giants of the volcanic world. They get their name from their broad, shield-like shape, which is due to the way they erupt. Instead of erupting explosively, shield volcanoes produce slow, steady streams of highly fluid lava that flows freely across the landscape. This lava travels farther than the stickier kind, leading to the growth of expansive, gently sloping sides over time.

Take Mauna Loa in Hawaii, for instance, the largest shield volcano on Earth. It's so wide that if you were standing on its summit, you wouldn't realize you were on a volcano at all! It would seem like a relatively flat landscape because the slopes are so gradual.

FUN FACT
Mauna Loa is so massive that if you measured from its true base on the ocean floor to its peak, it's actually taller than Mount Everest!

Explosive Stratovolcanoes

Stratovolcanoes, also known as composite volcanoes, are what most people envision when they think of volcanoes. These towering peaks have steep, conical shapes, and they're known for their explosive eruptions.

Why so explosive? It's all about the lava. The lava from stratovolcanoes is thicker and stickier than shield volcanoes, which means gases can't escape as easily. When pressure builds up from these trapped gases, BOOM! You get a dramatic, sometimes catastrophic, eruption.

Notable examples of stratovolcanoes include Mount Fuji in Japan and Mount St. Helens in the United States. The latter made headlines in 1980 with an eruption that blew off an entire side of the mountain.

FUN FACT

Mount Fuji, a stratovolcano, is Japan's tallest peak and a popular subject in Japanese art and culture. It's also considered an active volcano, though its last eruption was in 1707!

Popocatépetl is an active
stratovolcano
in Mexico.

Red Cinder Mountain, California. Image: Matthew Lee High

Simple Cinder Cones

Cinder cones, or scoria cones, are the simplest type of volcano. They're built from blobs of lava, called cinders, that are ejected from a single vent, fall back to Earth, and pile up around the vent. This results in a cone-shaped hill usually no more than a few hundred meters high.

Cinder cones have a bowl-shaped crater at the summit and rarely grow to the heights of shield or stratovolcanoes. However, they are often found on the flanks of these larger volcanoes. Parícutin in Mexico is a famous example of a cinder cone. It suddenly grew out of a cornfield in 1943 and reached its full height of 424 meters in just a year!

FUN FACT
The Earth's Moon has many cinder cones, formed by explosive eruptions of gas-rich lunar basalts!

Lava Domes

Lava domes are created when magma is too viscous (thick) to flow far away from the vent, causing the lava to pile up around the opening, forming a dome-like structure. These domes can be found on their own, or on the flanks and summits of stratovolcanoes. The magma of these domes contains more silica, making it thicker than the magma found in shield or cinder cone volcanoes.

FUN FACT

Mount St. Helens in the United States, known for its catastrophic eruption in 1980, has a lava dome in its crater, which you can see on the left. Over time, this dome has been growing taller and wider due to the slow oozing of magma from beneath the surface.

A fissure on Mauna Loa, Hawaii, erupting on December 1, 2022.

VOLCANOES BY ACTIVITY LEVEL

As well as their shape, Volcanoes are often classified by their level of activity. Understanding these levels is crucial for volcanologists as they monitor and predict volcanic behavior, helping to safeguard communities living near them.

Active Volcanoes

These are volcanoes that have erupted in the recent past and are expected to erupt again in the future. When we think of volcanoes, active volcanoes are often what come to mind - spewing lava, ash, and gases from their craters.

Examples include: Mauna Loa and Mount Kilauea in Hawaii, Mount Etna in Italy, and Mount St. Helens in the United States.

Dormant Volcanoes

A dormant volcano is like a sleeping giant. These volcanoes haven't erupted in a long time, but they aren't extinct. Given the right conditions, they could wake up and erupt again.

Examples include: Mount Fuji in Japan, Mount Rainier in the United States, and Teide in Spain.

Extinct Volcanoes

These are volcanoes that scientists consider unlikely to erupt again. They have no remaining lava supply and are often heavily eroded.

Examples include: the Edinburgh Castle in Scotland and Kilimanjaro in Tanzania (*pictured*).

Remember, while these categories are useful, nature doesn't always stick to the rules! Even dormant and extinct volcanoes need to be monitored as our understanding of volcanic activity continues to evolve.

HOW VOLCANOES ARE FORMED

THE EARTH'S LAYERS: SETTING THE STAGE

To understand how volcanoes are formed, we need to understand the structure of the Earth. Our planet is like a giant, spherical layer cake. It's made up of several layers: the **crust** (the part we live on), the **mantle** below it, and the **core** at the very center.

The crust and the upper part of the mantle form what's known as the lithosphere. This isn't one big piece, though—it's broken up into massive slabs called **tectonic plates**. These plates are constantly moving, albeit very slowly, due to the heat from the core and the lower part of the mantle.

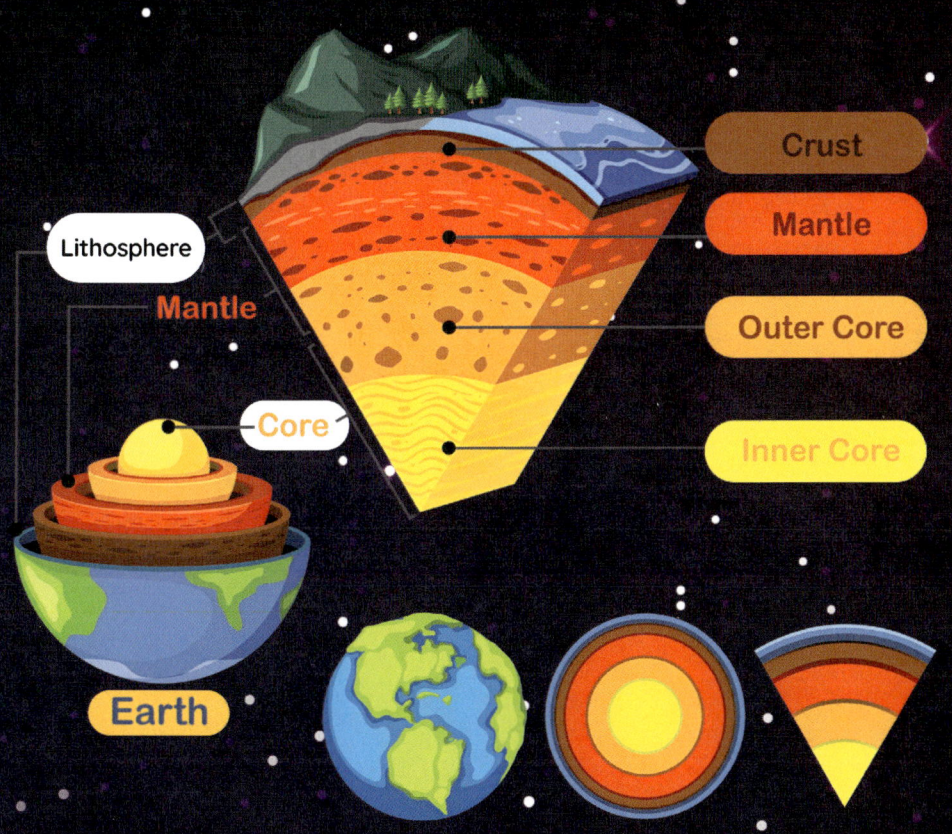

Lithosphere

Mantle

Core

Earth

Crust

Mantle

Outer Core

Inner Core

EARTH'S LAYERS

THE ROLE OF TECTONIC PLATES

The birth of a volcano is deeply connected to the movement of these tectonic plates. There are three main types of plate boundaries, each playing a distinct role in volcano formation. However, most volcanoes are found along convergent and divergent boundaries.

CONVERGENT BOUNDARIES occur when two plates collide or converge. When this happens, one plate often gets forced beneath the other in a process called **subduction**. The subducted plate heats up as it sinks into the mantle, melting into magma. This magma is less dense than the surrounding rock, so it rises, and if it breaks through the Earth's crust, a volcano forms.

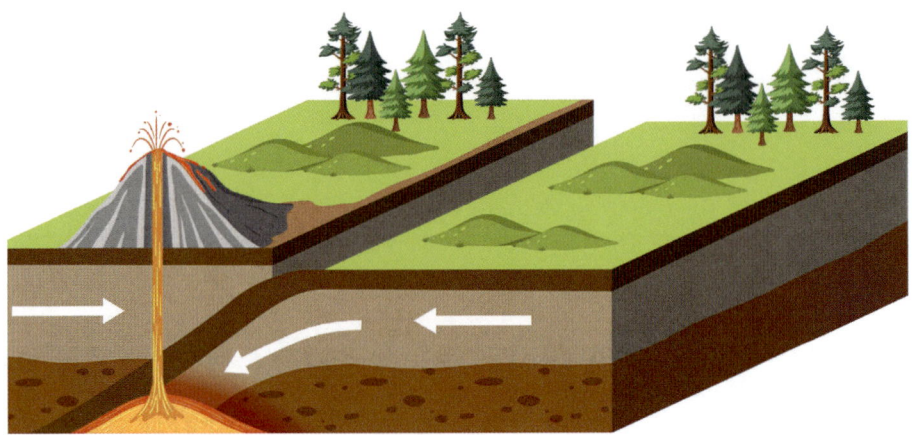

DIVERGENT BOUNDARIES are the opposite. Instead of coming together, these plates are moving apart. This happens at mid-ocean ridges, where new oceanic crust is being formed. The space created by the diverging plates allows magma to rise and form volcanoes.

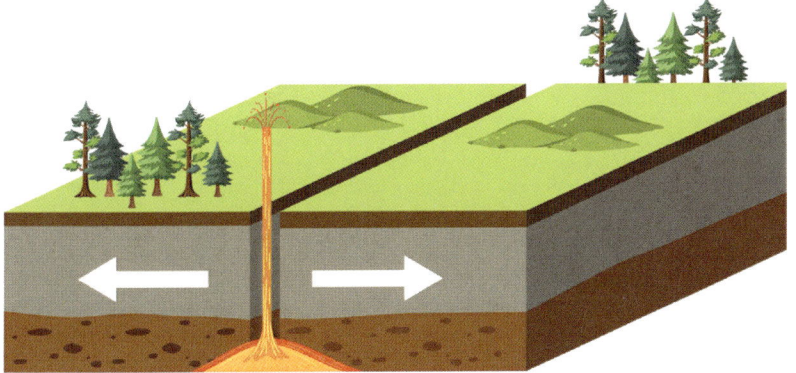

TRANSFORM BOUNDARIES occur when plates slide past each other horizontally. These aren't typically associated with volcanoes but are more known for causing earthquakes. However, in complex environments, volcanic activity can occur near these boundaries.

Bárðarbunga stratovolcano, Iceland

From Magma to Mountain: The Birth of a Volcano

So, we've got our magma, formed deep in the Earth. What happens next? Well, this is where our different types of volcanoes come back into the picture.

If the magma is low in silica, it's more fluid and can flow easily to the surface. This usually results in a gentle eruption and, over time, the formation of a shield volcano.

On the other hand, if the magma is high in silica, it's stickier and traps gases. The pressure from these trapped gases can lead to explosive eruptions, which are typical of stratovolcanoes and some cinder cones. Each eruption adds more material to the volcano, helping it to grow larger over time. Some volcanoes can even form in just a few months, while others take millions of years to reach their full size.

FUN FACT

Did you know that new islands can form from underwater volcanic eruptions? The island of Surtsey off the coast of Iceland was formed this way between 1963 and 1967!

INSIDE A
VOLCANO

Are you ready to take a plunge into the belly of a volcano? Don't worry, this is a metaphorical journey, so there's no need for fireproof gear or advanced scuba diving skills. Let's dive deep into what goes on inside a volcano.

THE MAGMA CHAMBER: WHERE IT ALL BEGINS

Imagine a vast, underground pool filled with incredibly hot, molten rock. This is the **magma chamber**, the heart of a volcano. Located in the Earth's crust or upper mantle, magma chambers collect magma that rises from deeper in the Earth. The size and location of magma chambers can vary greatly, but one thing is certain: without the magma chamber, there would be no volcano.

The magma within the chamber is under tremendous pressure, and it's this pressure that can cause an eruption when the magma forces its way to the surface. It's like shaking a soda can and then popping the top off—only on a much, much bigger scale!

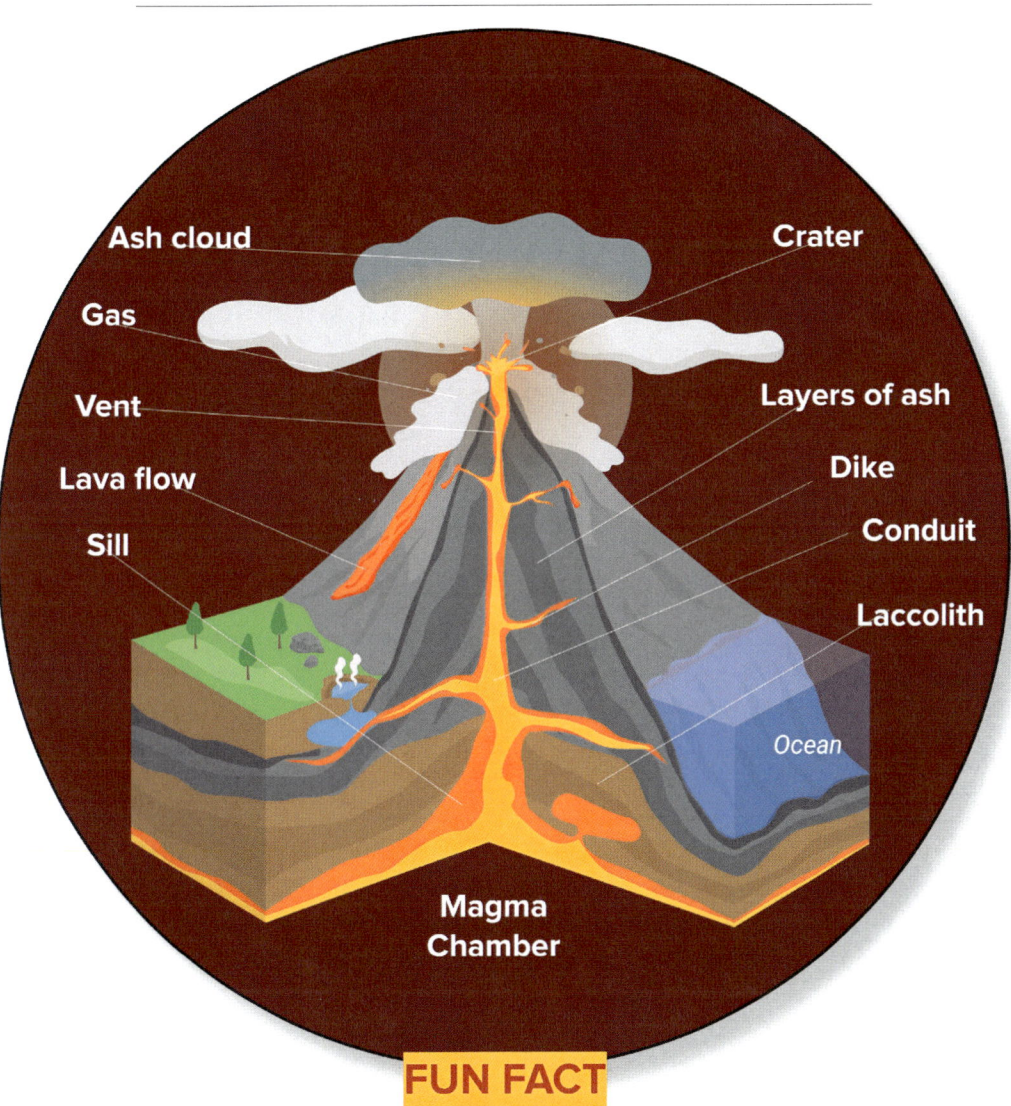

FUN FACT

The magma chamber beneath the Yellowstone National Park in the USA is one of the largest known. It's about 40 miles (64 km) wide and filled with enough magma to fill the Grand Canyon more than 11 times over!

FROM MAGMA TO LAVA: A FIERY TRANSFORMATION

So, what exactly is magma? It's a molten mixture of rock, crystals, and dissolved gases. And, as we mentioned in chapter one, once this magma reaches the surface, it becomes lava.

Different magmas produce different types of lava, which in turn create different types of eruptions and volcanoes. For example, 'pahoehoe' (say "pah-hoy-hoy") is a type of lava that cools into a smooth, ropey surface. Then there's 'aa' (pronounced "ah-ah") (*pictured left*), a slower-moving, chunky type of lava that cools into a jagged, rough surface.

FUN FACT
Some lava flows can reach speeds of up to 40 miles per hour (64 kilometers per hour)! That's faster than you'd cycle on a bike!

Pahoehoe rope lava in Hawai'i.

THE VOLCANIC VENTS: NATURE'S PRESSURE RELEASE

The vent is the part of the volcano where magma—now called lava—escapes. This can be a single spot, like the summit vent at the top of many volcanos, or a series of smaller vents, like the ones you'd find on the flanks of some shield volcanoes.

In some cases, the force of an eruption can create new vents in an existing volcano. During a flank eruption, for example, a new vent opens on the side of the volcano, providing an additional exit route for the pent-up magma.

THE VOLCANIC PLUMBING: CONDUITS, DIKES, LACCOLITHS & SILLS

But how does magma get from the magma chamber to the vent? The answer is through a complex "plumbing" system made up of conduits and dikes.

A **conduit** is the main "pipe" through which magma travels from the magma chamber to the vent.

During its journey, magma may encounter cracks and fissures in the surrounding rocks. Here, it forces itself into these weaknesses, forming **dikes**. Dikes are vertical or near-vertical sheets of magma, which

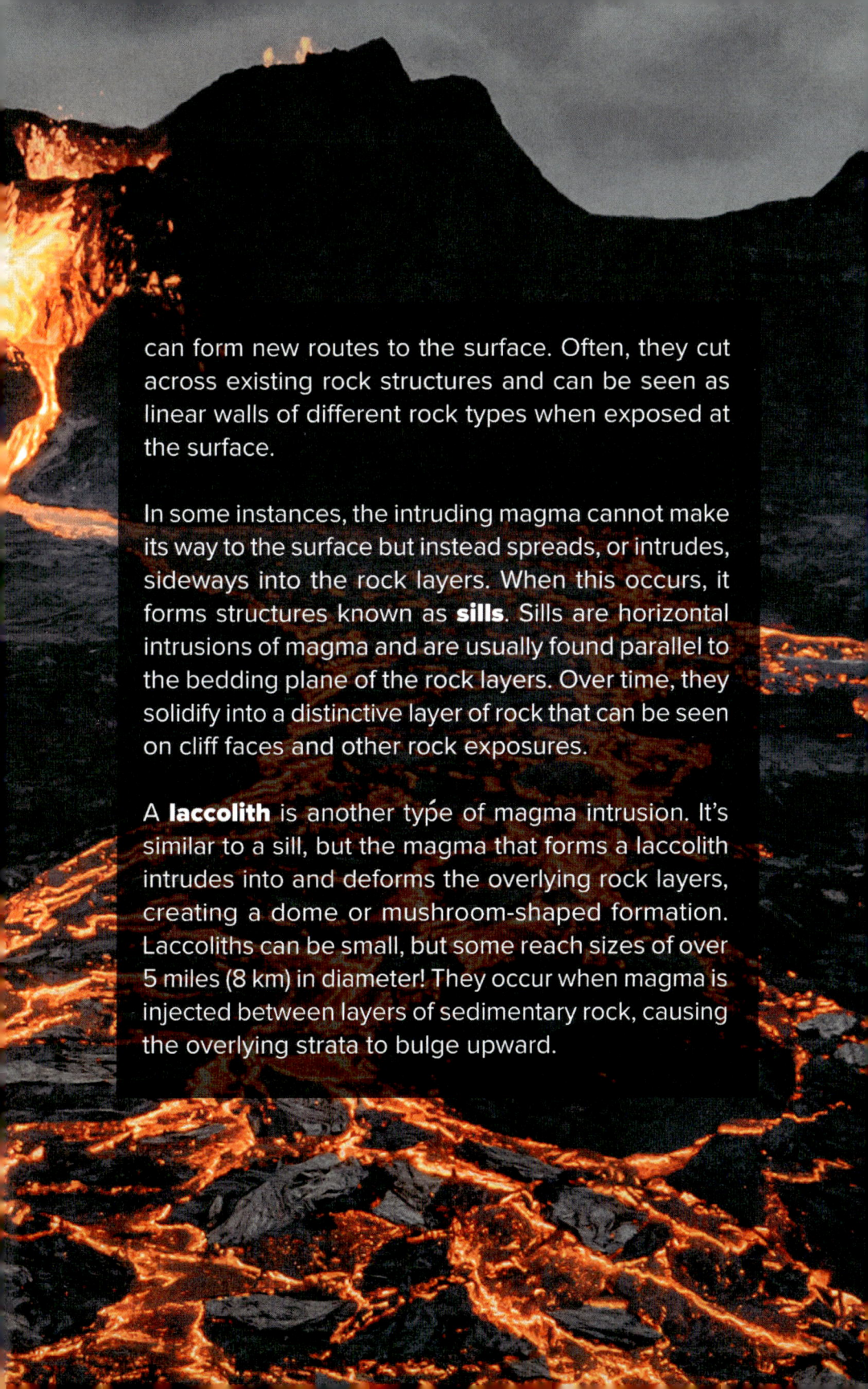

can form new routes to the surface. Often, they cut across existing rock structures and can be seen as linear walls of different rock types when exposed at the surface.

In some instances, the intruding magma cannot make its way to the surface but instead spreads, or intrudes, sideways into the rock layers. When this occurs, it forms structures known as **sills**. Sills are horizontal intrusions of magma and are usually found parallel to the bedding plane of the rock layers. Over time, they solidify into a distinctive layer of rock that can be seen on cliff faces and other rock exposures.

A **laccolith** is another type of magma intrusion. It's similar to a sill, but the magma that forms a laccolith intrudes into and deforms the overlying rock layers, creating a dome or mushroom-shaped formation. Laccoliths can be small, but some reach sizes of over 5 miles (8 km) in diameter! They occur when magma is injected between layers of sedimentary rock, causing the overlying strata to bulge upward.

Fagradalsfjall, Iceland.

THE ANATOMY OF AN ERUPTION

If a volcano is a sleeping dragon, then an eruption is when the dragon awakes! But, every dragon is different, and so is every volcanic eruption. So, what causes these explosive events, and what happens when a volcano blows its top? Let's find out.

WHAT TRIGGERS AN ERUPTION?

First, we need to understand what causes a volcano to erupt. The main driving force is the **magma**. Remember how we talked about the pressure building up in the magma chamber? When the pressure from the gases within the magma becomes too high, the magma forces its way to the surface, leading to an eruption. But, not all eruptions are the same. The style of an eruption depends on the magma's composition—particularly its silica content and the amount of dissolved gases it contains.

Silica makes magma sticky or viscous, which traps gases. High-silica magma often leads to explosive eruptions, while low-silica magma can flow out smoothly. The higher the gas content, the more explosive the eruption can be.

DIFFERENT ERUPTION STYLES AND CHARACTERISTICS

There are several types of volcanic eruptions, each with its unique features and behaviors.

EFFUSIVE ERUPTIONS are gentle eruptions where lava steadily flows out of the volcano. This type of eruption is common in shield volcanoes, where the low-silica lava can flow freely.

An effusive eruption at the west vent in Halemaʻumaʻu crater at the summit of Kīlauea.

STROMBOLIAN ERUPTIONS are named after the Stromboli volcano in Italy (*left*), which has been erupting almost continuously for over 2,000 years! These eruptions are like a fireworks display, with bright, glowing blobs of lava shot into the sky.

EXPLOSIVE ERUPTIONS, are very violent and can blast ash and rock fragments called **tephra** into the air. The lava is high in silica, which makes it too sticky to flow smoothly. Pressure builds up until it's released in a massive explosion. Stratovolcanoes often have explosive eruptions.

One type of explosive eruption is called the Plinian eruption, which is the most powerful. The eruptions of Mount St. Helens in 1980 (*right*) and Mount Vesuvius in 79 AD are examples of Plinian eruptions.

FUN FACT

Some eruptions are so powerful they can be heard hundreds of miles away! The 1883 eruption of Krakatoa in Indonesia was heard over 1,900 miles (3,000 km) away.

THE VOLCANIC EXPLOSIVITY INDEX (VEI)

To compare the size or power of different volcanic eruptions, scientists use the **Volcanic Explosivity Index**, or VEI. It's like the Richter scale for earthquakes, but for volcanic eruptions!

The VEI is a scale from 0 to 8 that measures the amount of volcanic material ejected, the height of the eruption column, and how long the eruption lasts. A VEI of 0 is a gentle, non-explosive eruption, while a VEI of 8 is a colossal eruption that can affect the global climate. On the right, you can see the VEI of some of the most famous volcanic eruptions.

FUN FACT

The eruption of Mount Tambora in Indonesia in 1815 is the only eruption in recorded history to reach a VEI of 7. This eruption caused what became known as "the year without a summer" across the globe due to its impact on climate.

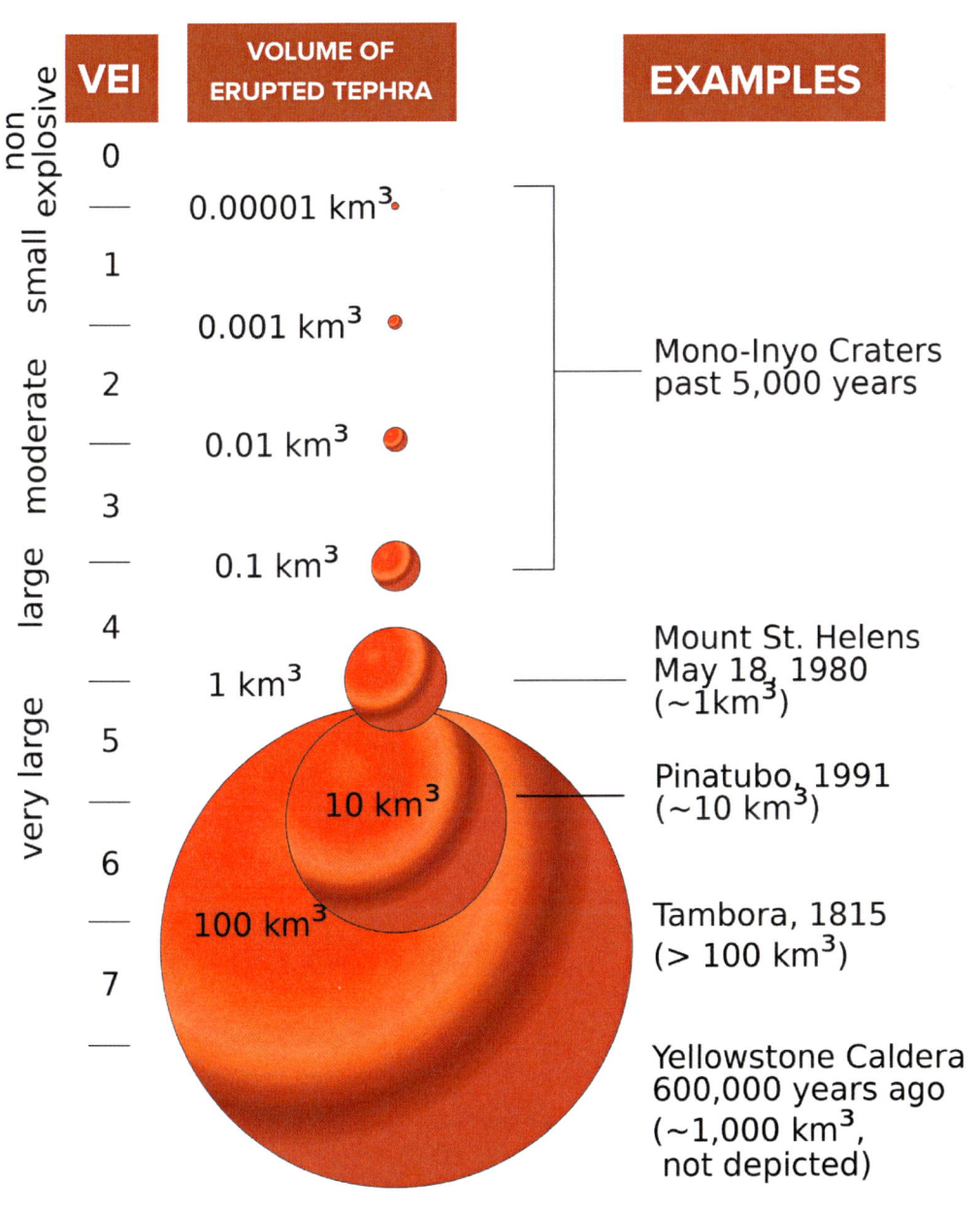

VEI

VOLUME OF ERUPTED TEPHRA

EXAMPLES

non explosive — 0

small — 1
0.00001 km³

2
0.001 km³

moderate — 3
0.01 km³

Mono-Inyo Craters past 5,000 years

large — 4
0.1 km³

1 km³

Mount St. Helens May 18, 1980 (~1km³)

very large — 5

10 km³

Pinatubo, 1991 (~10 km³)

6

100 km³

Tambora, 1815 (> 100 km³)

7

Yellowstone Caldera 600,000 years ago (~1,000 km³, not depicted)

FAMOUS HISTORICAL ERUPTIONS

Volcanic eruptions can leave a significant mark on history, and some have become legendary!

Take **MOUNT VESUVIUS**, for instance. Its eruption in 79 AD buried the bustling Roman cities of Pompeii and Herculaneum, preserving them under a thick layer of ash. Today, these sites offer a time capsule into life during Roman times.

The 1883 eruption of **KRAKATOA** is another infamous event. It was one of the deadliest and most destructive volcanic events in recorded history, causing tsunamis and leading to thousands of deaths.

Lastly, the 1980 eruption of **MOUNT ST. HELENS** in Washington, USA, was the most destructive in the country's history. It caused a massive landslide and killed 57 people, showing the devastating power of volcanoes.

In the next chapter, we'll take a world tour of volcanoes. From the fiery ring of the Pacific to the frozen landscape of Iceland, get ready to embark on an adventure to the most fascinating volcanic regions of the world!

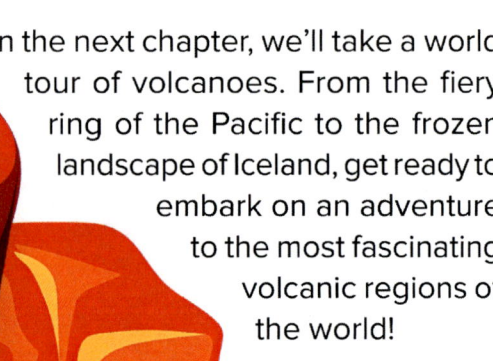

Mount St. Helens the day before the eruption (above), and two years later (below). Notice the large crater and lava dome.

VOLCANOES
AROUND THE WORLD

Ready for a global adventure? From the icy vistas of Iceland to the tropical paradise of Hawaii, volcanoes have created some of the most breathtaking landscapes on our planet. In this chapter, we'll travel around the world, exploring famous volcanic hotspots and regions. Let's go!

FUN FACT

Hawaii's Kilauea volcano, part of the Pacific ring of fire, is one of the most active volcanoes on Earth. Its recent eruption in 2018 resulted in more than a dozen lava flows that reached the ocean, adding new land to the island.

**Mount Masaraga,
Philippines**

THE PACIFIC RING OF FIRE: A CIRCLE OF FURY

Our first stop is the Pacific Ring of Fire, an area known for its frequent earthquakes and volcanic activity. This massive ring stretches 25,000 miles (40,000 kilometers) and includes 452 volcanoes—about 75% of the world's active volcanoes!

The Ring of Fire is home to some of the world's most famous and active volcanoes, including Mount St. Helens in the United States, Mount Fuji in Japan, and Mount Pinatubo in the Philippines. Remember, this region is a hotspot due to the many tectonic plate boundaries—both convergent and divergent—found here.

VOLCANOES OF THE MEDITERRANEAN: CRADLE OF MYTHOLOGY

Our next stop is the Mediterranean, home to some of the world's most legendary volcanoes. Mount Etna in Sicily (*pictured*) is Europe's tallest active volcano and one of the most active in the world. Then there's the famous Mount Vesuvius, the only active volcano on the European mainland.

It's no surprise that these fiery mountains had a profound impact on the ancient cultures living in their shadow. Many myths and legends were inspired by their eruptions—like the idea that the god of fire, Hephaestus (or Vulcan in Roman), had his forge under Mount Etna.

ICELAND: THE LAND OF FIRE AND ICE

Next, we're off to Iceland, a country that truly lives up to its nickname: the land of fire and ice. This small island has around 30 active volcanic systems! The reason? It's located on the Mid-Atlantic Ridge, a divergent tectonic boundary where the North American and Eurasian plates are pulling apart.

One of the most famous Icelandic volcanoes is Eyjafjallajökull. Remember the big eruption in 2010 that caused chaos for air travel across Europe? That was Eyjafjallajökull!

A volcanic eruption at Geldingadalir, Fagradalsfjall, Iceland.

FUN FACT

Did you know that a new ocean is forming in the East African Rift Valley? In millions of years, East Africa could split from the rest of the continent to form a new landmass!

THE AFRICAN RIFT VALLEY: A CONTINENT SPLITTING APART

Our final stop is the East African Rift Valley. Stretching over 3,000 miles (4,828 kilometers) from Jordan in Southwest Asia to Mozambique in Southeast Africa, this region is a divergent plate boundary where the African Plate is splitting apart.

This tectonic activity has resulted in some truly spectacular volcanoes, like Ol Doinyo Lengai in Tanzania (*pictured*), which is unique because it produces the coolest and most alkaline lava in the world.

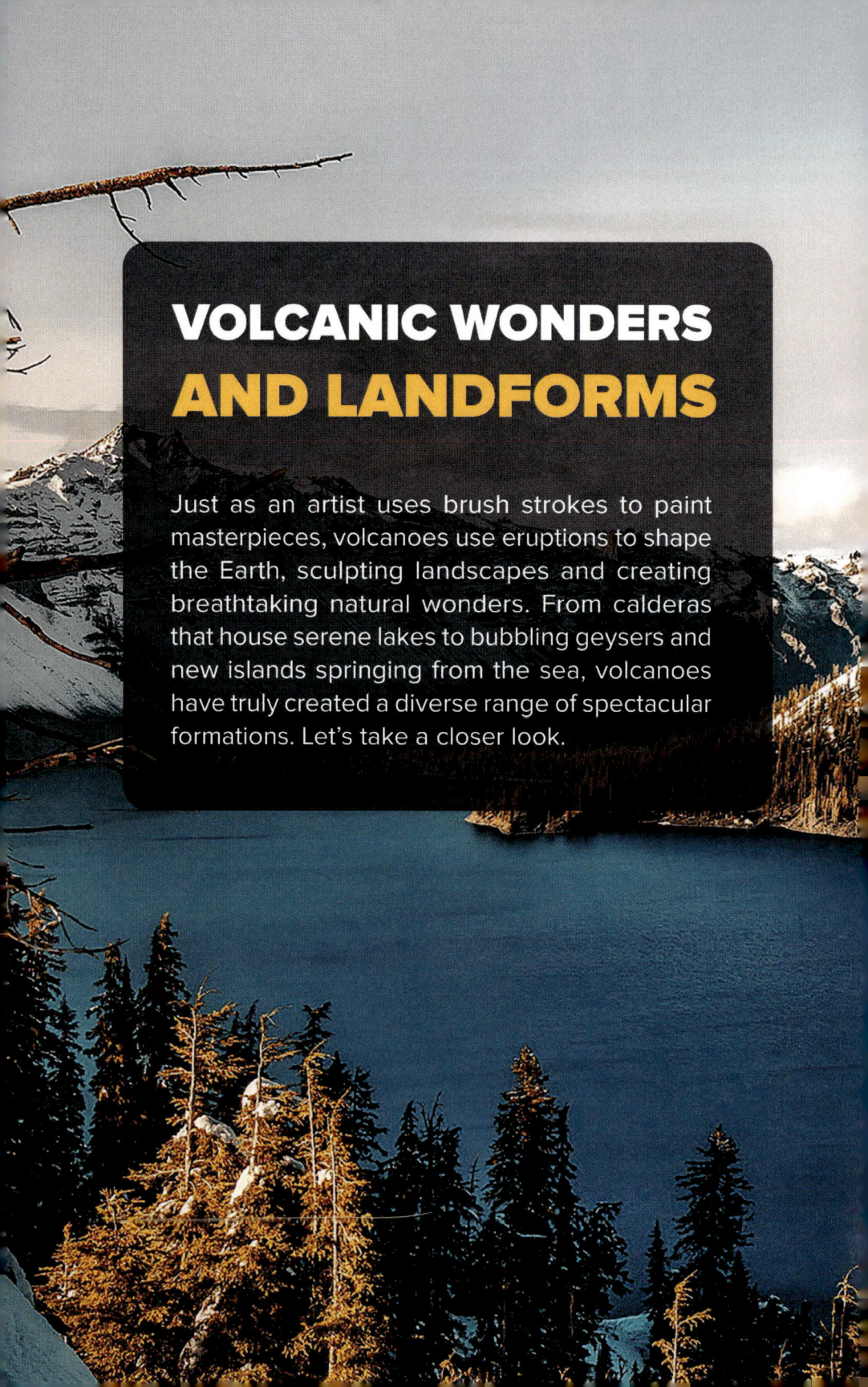

VOLCANIC WONDERS
AND LANDFORMS

Just as an artist uses brush strokes to paint masterpieces, volcanoes use eruptions to shape the Earth, sculpting landscapes and creating breathtaking natural wonders. From calderas that house serene lakes to bubbling geysers and new islands springing from the sea, volcanoes have truly created a diverse range of spectacular formations. Let's take a closer look.

CALDERAS: MORE THAN JUST A CRATER

First, let's delve into the world of calderas. These are gigantic, bowl-shaped depressions that form when a volcano erupts so violently it collapses in on itself. They're like craters, but on a much larger scale.

One of the most famous calderas is at Yellowstone National Park in the United States. But don't expect to see a massive hole in the ground—it's so large that you'd be inside it without even knowing! Calderas often fill with water over time, creating beautiful lakes, like Oregon's Crater Lake (*pictured*) and Santorini's caldera in Greece.

FUN FACT

The word 'caldera' comes from the Spanish word for 'cauldron'. A fitting name, don't you think?

LAVA LAKES AND GEYSERS: NATURE'S HOT TUBS

Next up are lava lakes and geysers, two geological features that showcase the intense heat beneath the Earth's surface.

Lava lakes are large, pool-like reservoirs of molten lava. They're incredibly rare—there are only seven in the world—and can mostly be found in shield volcanoes, like those in Hawaii and the Democratic Republic of Congo. There is also one in Antarctica.

Geysers are different but no less fascinating. They're essentially hot springs that periodically erupt, shooting water and steam into the air. The most famous geyser is probably Old Faithful (*pictured*) in Yellowstone National Park, known for its highly predictable eruptions.

Lava Lake Nyiragongo, DRC

Kauai, Hawaii.

VOLCANIC ISLANDS AND ARCHIPELAGOS: BIRTH OF LAND

Our journey takes us now to the ocean. Remember Hawaii? It's a great example of a volcanic archipelago, a group of islands formed by volcanic activity.

Volcanic islands and archipelagos form some of the most fascinating and diverse ecosystems on our planet. But how do these isolated landmasses rise from the depths of the sea? Let's delve deeper into the extraordinary processes that give birth to these lands.

The Formation Process

Volcanic islands typically form at tectonic plate boundaries—either where plates are moving apart (divergent boundaries) or coming together (convergent boundaries).

At divergent boundaries, such as the Mid-Atlantic Ridge, magma rises to fill the gap as the plates move apart. The magma hardens as it reaches the cold ocean water, creating a new seabed. Over thousands of years, repeated eruptions can build up enough material to break the ocean surface and form an island.

At convergent boundaries, one tectonic plate slides beneath another in a process called subduction. This generates intense heat and pressure, melting the subducting plate and creating magma. This magma can rise and erupt on the ocean floor, forming seamounts. If these underwater volcanoes grow large enough to reach the ocean's surface, they form volcanic islands.

A Tour of Notable Volcanic Islands and Archipelagos

As we've already mentioned, Hawaii and the Galapagos Islands are fantastic examples of volcanic archipelagos. Let's explore a few more.

THE ALEUTIAN ISLANDS: This chain of 14 large volcanic islands and 55 smaller ones forms a bridge between North America and Asia. These islands are part of the Pacific Ring of Fire and sit on a subduction zone, where the Pacific Plate dives beneath the North American Plate.

THE CANARY ISLANDS: Off the northwest coast of Africa, these Spanish islands are another example of a volcanic archipelago. Tenerife, the largest island, is home to Mount Teide (*pictured*), the third tallest volcano in the world when measured from its base on the ocean floor.

Aegean Sea is the remnant of a much larger landmass that was mostly destroyed by a colossal volcanic eruption around 1600 BCE. Today, Santorini's stunning cliffside towns overlook a water-filled caldera—the scar left by the ancient eruption.

FUN FACT

Despite being thousands of miles away, the eruption that formed Santorini's caldera may have influenced the legend of Atlantis, the mythical city said to have sunk beneath the waves overnight.

SURTSEY, ICELAND: This island, born from a four-year-long undersea eruption that started in 1963, is one of the youngest landmasses on Earth. It's been closely studied by scientists to understand how life colonizes new lands.

Volcanic islands and archipelagos are testament to the raw power of volcanic forces. Not only do they offer spectacular landscapes and rich biodiversity, but they also provide scientists with invaluable insights into geological processes and the evolution of life.

THE GOOD AND THE BAD OF VOLCANOES

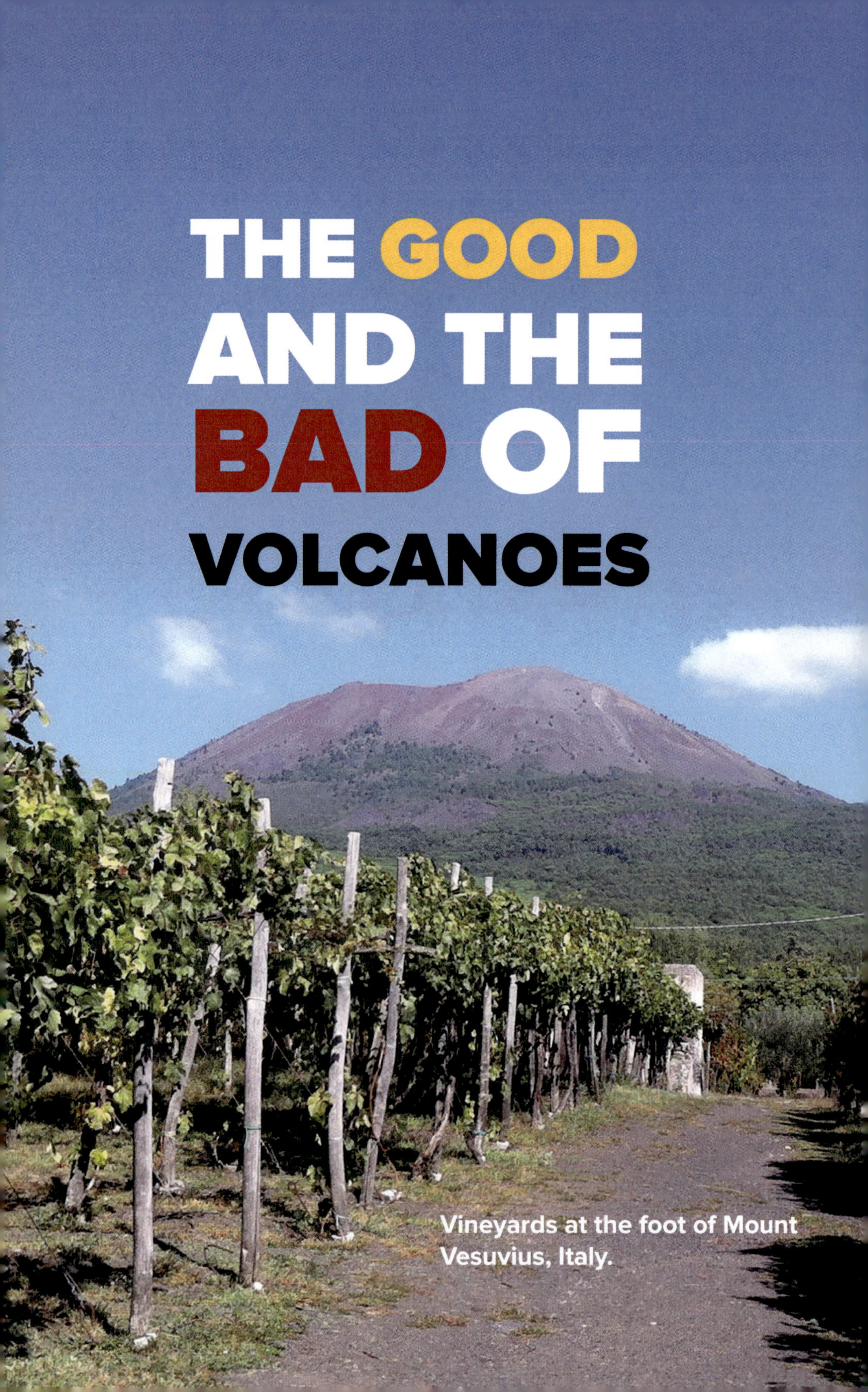

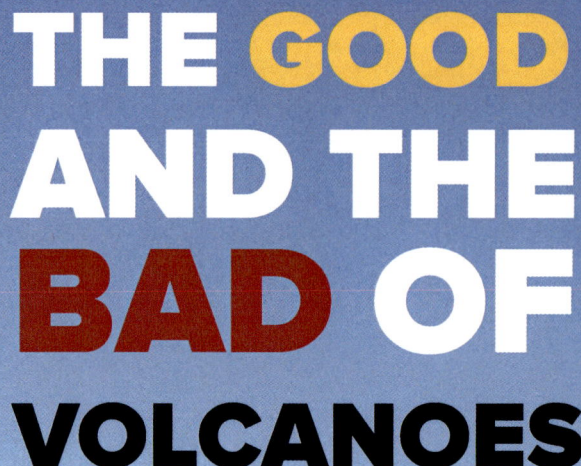

Vineyards at the foot of Mount Vesuvius, Italy.

As we've explored the world of volcanoes, it's clear that they can be both awe-inspiring and fear-inducing. Their eruptions have shaped landscapes, built islands, and created amazing features like calderas and lava tubes. But, they can also cause destruction and pose dangers to human life and the environment. Let's dive into both the advantages and perils associated with volcanoes.

BENEFITS: FERTILE SOIL, GEOTHERMAL ENERGY, AND TOURISM

Despite their destructive potential, volcanoes offer numerous benefits. It's their way of giving back, we suppose.

Fertile Soil: The Life-Bearing Ash

One of the most significant benefits of volcanic eruptions is the creation of incredibly fertile soil. When a volcano erupts, it releases ash loaded with nutrients beneficial to plants. As the ash mixes with the soil, it enhances the soil's fertility, making it perfect for farming. Areas around Mount Vesuvius in Italy, for example, are renowned for their rich vineyards and tomato crops. And coffee beans grown in volcanic soil? Some of the best in the world!

Geothermal Energy: Harnessing Earth's Heat

Did you know that volcanoes can help generate electricity? Regions with high volcanic activity often have substantial geothermal energy potential. This is heat energy from within the Earth, often associated with magma. By drilling into the Earth's crust in these areas, we can tap into this heat and use it to produce electricity. Countries like Iceland and the Philippines use geothermal power to supply a significant portion of their energy needs.

Tourism: An Explosive Attraction

Lastly, volcanoes draw in tourists from all over the world, contributing to local economies. Who wouldn't want to hike up a volcano or explore a lava tube? Whether it's Hawaii Volcanoes National Park in the USA, Mount Fuji in Japan, or the stunning caldera of Santorini in Greece, these fiery giants offer incredible opportunities for adventure and learning.

FUN FACT

Krafla power station (pictured) is a geothermal powerstation in Iceland. Around 89% of houses in Iceland are heated by geothermal energy!

HAZARDS: LAVA FLOWS, ASH CLOUDS, AND LAHARS

But along with the good comes the bad. Volcanoes pose significant hazards, not only during an eruption but also afterwards.

Lava Flows: Rivers of Fire

One of the most iconic dangers associated with volcanoes is the flow of lava. When a volcano erupts, it can release a river of molten rock that incinerates everything in its path. While most lava flows move slowly, giving people enough time to evacuate, they can still cause massive property damage.

Ash Clouds: The Sky Darkens

Volcanic ash isn't like the ash you'd find in a barbecue. It's tiny jagged pieces of rock and glass that can be harmful to breathe, damaging to aircraft engines, and disruptive to daily life. Large ash clouds (right) can even affect global climate by blocking out sunlight.

A lahar travels through a town after the 1995 eruption of Mt. Pinatubo, Philippines.

Lahars: Deadly Mudslides

Perhaps less known but incredibly dangerous are lahars, which are volcanic mudflows or debris flows. A lahar occurs when volcanic ash and other material become saturated with water from heavy rains or the melting of a volcano's ice cap, causing a torrent of slurry to rush down the slopes. Lahars can move at high speeds and wipe out entire communities, like in the tragic 1985 eruption of Nevado del Ruiz in Colombia.

A volcanologist inspects a new eruption in Halemaʻumaʻu crater, in January 2023.

HEROES OF HEAT:
VOLCANOLOGISTS

Who wouldn't want to study something as awesome as volcanoes, right? Well, for those brave enough to tackle the heat, dust, and occasional need to run very fast, there's a whole career field ready to welcome you: volcanology. These intrepid individuals, armed with knowledge and sophisticated technology, help us understand volcanoes better. Let's explore their exciting world!

THE ROLE OF VOLCANOLOGISTS

Volcanologists are the superheroes of the geological world, risking their lives to understand one of nature's most awe-inspiring phenomena. But what exactly do they do?

Volcanologists study how volcanoes form, their eruption styles, the effects of their eruptions, and, importantly, how to predict their next big show. By studying past eruptions, they can forecast future ones, helping protect people and property.

TOOLS AND EQUIPMENT USED TO STUDY VOLCANOES

Volcanologists use a variety of tools and technologies in their work. Here are some of the most crucial ones:

Seismometers: Listening to the Earth's Tremors

Seismometers detect and record the Earth's movements, including those caused by volcanic activity. By studying these seismic waves, volcanologists can identify signs that magma is on the move.

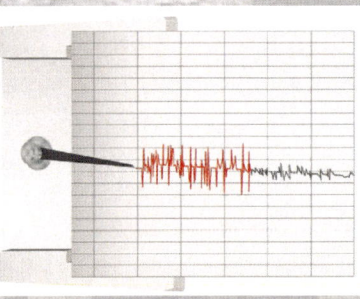

Gas Sensors: Sniffing Out Eruptions

As magma rises, it releases gases. Monitoring these gases can help predict an eruption. For example, an increase in sulfur dioxide might indicate that magma is nearing the surface.

A volcanologist collects lava samples in Hawaii.

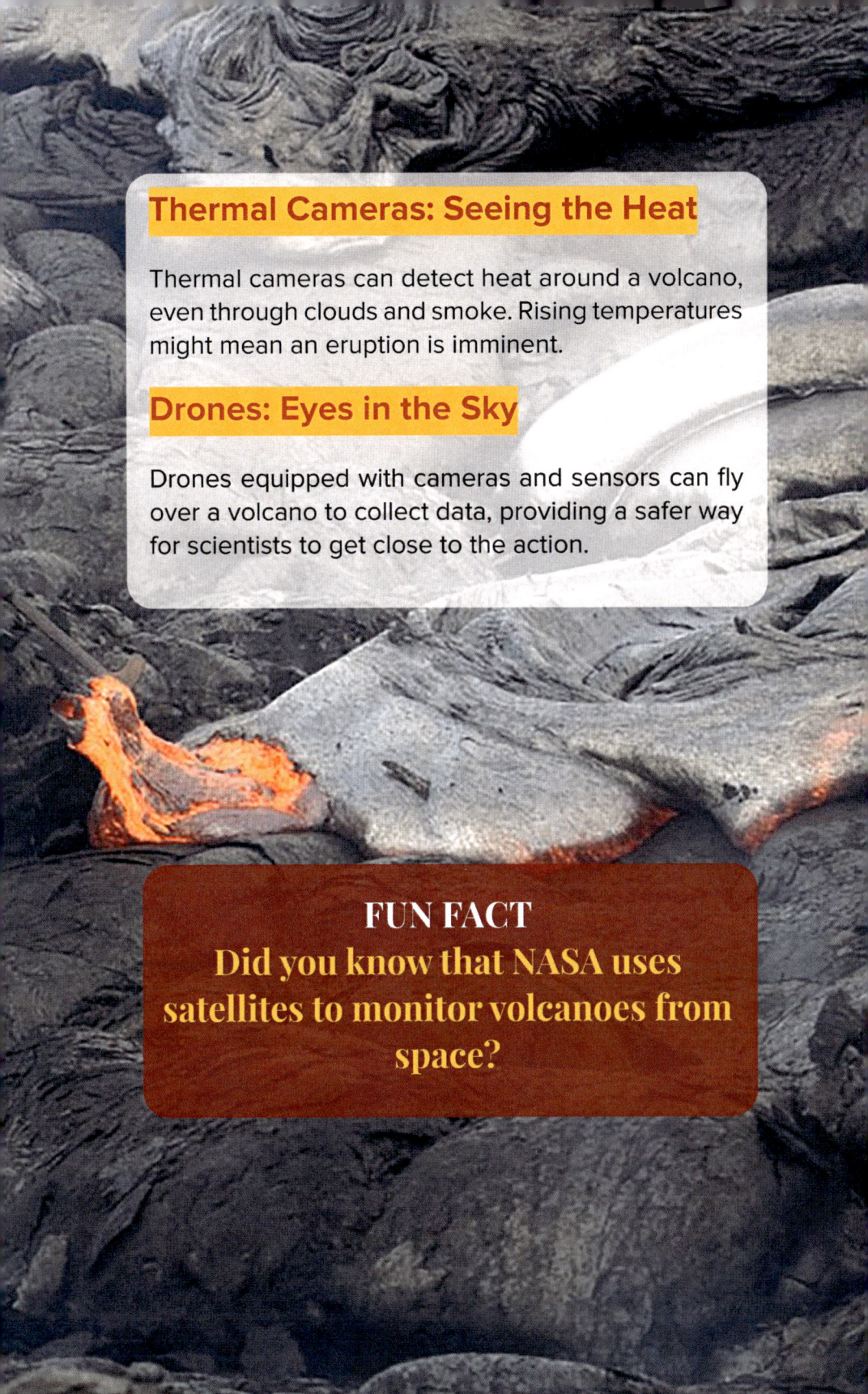

Thermal Cameras: Seeing the Heat

Thermal cameras can detect heat around a volcano, even through clouds and smoke. Rising temperatures might mean an eruption is imminent.

Drones: Eyes in the Sky

Drones equipped with cameras and sensors can fly over a volcano to collect data, providing a safer way for scientists to get close to the action.

FUN FACT
Did you know that NASA uses satellites to monitor volcanoes from space?

PROTECTING OUR
PLANET AND
OURSELVES

After exploring the world of volcanoes — their formation, types, the role they've played in shaping landscapes, and their cultural impact — we come to a crucial question: how do we live safely with these fiery forces of nature? The key lies in understanding, preparing, and respecting their power. So, let's dive into our final chapter.

MONITORING AND PREDICTING VOLCANIC ERUPTIONS

One of the main ways we protect ourselves from volcanic hazards is through careful monitoring and prediction. Remember our volcano superheroes, the volcanologists? They're on the frontline here, employing a variety of techniques and tools.

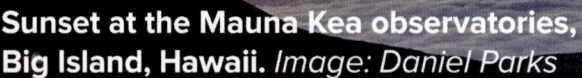

Sunset at the Mauna Kea observatories, Big Island, Hawaii. *Image: Daniel Parks*

Stationed strategically near some of the world's most active volcanoes, these observatories act as nerve centers for monitoring volcanic activity. They are equipped with a range of tools - from gas sensors that detect changes in gas levels, indicating magma movement, to ground deformation tools and satellite imagery that track subtle changes in the volcano's shape, a sign of magma build-up.

These observatories also serve as research centers, where scientists meticulously study a volcano's eruption history. By combining data from past eruptions with real-time monitoring, they can better predict future eruptions and issue timely warnings.

PREPARING FOR VOLCANIC DISASTERS

Preparation is another critical part of protecting ourselves from volcanic threats. This includes creating evacuation plans, building infrastructure designed to withstand volcanic hazards, and educating communities about what to do before, during, and after an eruption.

For example, some towns located near active volcanoes have designated evacuation routes and shelters. Schools and local organizations often conduct drills so that everyone knows what to do if an eruption occurs.

Remember: If you live near a volcano or are visiting one, always stay informed about its status and follow instructions from local authorities.

FUN FACT

There's a Volcano Alert Level system, ranging from "Normal" (green) to "Warning" (red), to keep the public informed about a volcano's status.

THE IMPACT OF VOLCANOES ON CLIMATE AND THE ENVIRONMENT

Volcanoes aren't just a local concern. They can have global effects, particularly on our climate and environment. Large volcanic eruptions can blast millions of tons of gas and ash into the atmosphere, which can affect global temperatures and weather patterns.

Ash and sulfur dioxide can form an aerosol veil in the stratosphere, reflecting sunlight and causing global cooling.

But it's not all bad news. Volcanic gases like carbon dioxide contribute to the carbon cycle, and volcanic soil can support rich ecosystems. Understanding these effects can guide us in managing our environment and adapting to climate changes.

Mount Penanjakan, Indonesia.

VOLCANO FUN FACTS

Just when you thought you knew all there is to know about volcanoes, we're turning up the heat with some scorching trivia.

A volcanic lightning phenomenon known as a "dirty thunderstorm" can occur during eruptions.

●●●

The world's deepest volcano is the West Mata in the Pacific Ocean; it's located almost 4,000 ft (1,219 m) below sea level.

●●●

Volcanoes exist not just on Earth, but on other planets and moons too. For example, Olympus Mons on Mars is the largest volcano in our solar system, standing at a whopping 22 km (13.6 miles) high.

The word "volcano" originally comes from "Vulcano," a volcanic island in Italy that was named after Vulcan, the Roman god of fire.

●●●

The average temperature of lava is between 1,300 and 2,200 degrees Fahrenheit (704 to 1,204 degrees Celsius).

●●●

Some underwater volcanoes can create "fire fountains" under the sea due to the pressure of water and gas.

●●●

There's a volcano in Indonesia that spews blue lava. It's called Kawah Ijen (*below*), and the blue color comes from burning sulfur.

The fastest lava flow recorded was during the 1959 eruption of Kilauea Iki in Hawaii, clocking speeds of up to 60 km/h (37 mph).

●●●

Volcanic ash is very fine and can travel hundreds of miles.

●●●

"Pillow lava" is a unique type of lava that forms underwater, creating rounded shapes that look like pillows.

●●●

The ash cloud from the 2010 eruption of Eyjafjallajökull in Iceland caused the largest air-traffic shut-down since World War II.

●●●

Mount Kilimanjaro in Tanzania has three volcanic cones. Two of them are extinct, but one is still dormant, meaning it could erupt in the future.

●●●

The 1883 eruption of Krakatoa in Indonesia was so loud it was heard over 3,000 miles away.

"Extinct" volcanoes are those that haven't erupted in tens of thousands of years and are unlikely to ever erupt again.

●●●

Lava tubes can be several meters to several kilometers long.

●●●

The Yellowstone Caldera in Wyoming is known as a "supervolcano" due to its potential to produce extremely large eruptions.

●●●

In the Philippines, there is a remarkable lake called Taal lake (seen left). Within the lake, there is a volcano known as Taal volcano. And guess what? Inside the crater of Taal volcano, there is yet another lake, which has its very own island. It's like a lake within a volcano within a lake.

More than half of the world's active volcanoes above sea level are part of the Ring of Fire.

•••

Volcanic gas is mostly water vapor, followed by carbon dioxide and sulfur dioxide.

•••

Cinder cones are the simplest type of volcano, built from blobs of lava ejected from a single vent.

•••

The color of volcanic rocks can tell you about their composition: dark-colored rocks are called "mafic," and light-colored ones are called "felsic."

•••

The soil around volcanoes is very fertile, making regions near active volcanoes excellent for farming.

•••

Lava flows can reach the ocean and create new land. Pictured behind is lava from Kilauea on Hawaii flowing into the ocean in 2017.

When an underwater volcano erupts, it can create a new island.

•••

Volcanoes can form in the middle of a tectonic plate, where magma rises in "hot spots."

•••

Scientists can use ice cores to find evidence of past volcanic eruptions.

•••

The viscous lava of composite volcanoes can create impressive "lava domes."

•••

The Laki eruption in Iceland (1783-1784) had significant effects on global climate and caused a famine that led to the French Revolution.

•••

The Siberian Traps in Russia are the largest volcanic region on Earth.

Yellowstone National Park in the USA is actually an active volcanic system.

• • ▪

Volcanoes can sometimes form "volcanic plugs" – solidified lava that blocks the vent after an eruption.

• • ●

Sometimes, gases trapped in magma can cause "lava fountains" during an eruption.

• • ●

Some volcanoes are named after their distinct shape. For instance, "Maar" volcanoes are named after a German term for "sea," because they leave behind a round, lake-filled crater.

• • ●

The biggest volcano on Earth, Mauna Loa in Hawaii, is still considered active. Its last eruption was in 1984.

• • ●

Scientists sometimes use drones to study volcanoes closely without risking human life.

Mount Bromo, Indonesia.

The country with the most volcanoes is Indonesia, with over 130 active volcanoes.

● ● ●

The oldest volcano is thought to be Etna, which is about 350,000 years old.

● ● ●

"Cryovolcanoes" or "ice volcanoes" can be found on some icy moons in our solar system. They spew out water, ammonia, or methane instead of molten rock.

● ● ●

Pumice, a type of volcanic rock, is the only rock that can float on water.

● ● ●

The biggest volcanic eruption in recorded history was the 1815 eruption of Mount Tambora in Indonesia, which led to the "Year Without a Summer."

● ● ●

The Parícutin volcano in Mexico is one of the few volcanoes that humans have witnessed forming from its birth.

Some people bake bread in the naturally heated ground in regions with high volcanic activity, like in Iceland.

●●●

The largest volcano in Europe is Mount Etna in Sicily, Italy.

●●●

A volcano's "crater" is the bowl-shaped hole at the top. If it's more than 1 km in diameter, it's called a "caldera."

●●●

The tallest volcano in Japan, Mount Fuji, is a symbol of the country.

●●●

A "lava plateau" is formed when a lot of lava pours out of a fissure on the Earth's surface, spreads out, and cools.

●●●

The volcanic island of Surtsey in Iceland was declared a UNESCO World Heritage site in 2008.

Mount Fuji, Japan.

A "volcanic bomb" is a chunk of lava that cools into a rock before it hits the ground.

•••

Some volcanoes can have eruptions that last for years. The Stromboli volcano in Italy has been continuously erupting for over 2,000 years.

•••

Magma that's rich in silica tends to be more viscous and can lead to explosive eruptions.

•••

Volcanic ash can be harmful to inhale and can contaminate water supplies.

•••

The Roman city of Pompeii (*pictured*) was buried under meters of ash and pumice after the catastrophic eruption of Mount Vesuvius in 79 AD.

Some species of plants and animals have adapted to life in volcanic areas.

●●●

Scientists estimate that there are about 1,500 potentially active volcanoes worldwide.

●●●

When lava cools rapidly, it can form a type of glass called "obsidian" (*right*).

●●●

Some types of fish thrive in the hot, acidic water around underwater hydrothermal vents.

●●●

Magma chambers can be as small as a kilometer across, or as large as tens of kilometers.

●●●

The explosive eruption of Krakatoa in 1883 generated a tsunami that killed over 36,000 people.

The eruption of Novarupta in Alaska in 1912 was the largest of the 20th century.

•••

Mauna Kea, a volcano on the Big Island of Hawaii, is technically the tallest mountain in the world if measured from its base beneath the ocean.

•••

In Guatemala, you can roast marshmallows over the heat of the active Pacaya volcano (*see picture*).

•••

During the Ice Age, melting ice caused by volcanic heat helped to form many caves around the world.

•••

Basalt is the most common type of volcanic rock, and makes up most of the ocean floor.

•••

The Columbia River Plateau in the western United States was formed by a series of massive lava flows.

The temperature of the Earth's interior increases by about 1.8 degrees Fahrenheit (1 degree Celsius) every 131 feet (40 m) down you go — that's called the geothermal gradient.

•••

A "lava tree" forms when lava coats a tree, the tree burns away, and a cast of the tree is left in the hardened lava.

•••

"Scoria" is a type of volcanic rock that forms when blobs of gas-charged lava explode and cool.

•••

Mount Pelee on the island of Martinique had the deadliest eruption of the 20th century, killing around 30,000 people in 1902.

•••

Underwater volcanoes, or "seamounts," outnumber those on land.

•••

There are more than 500 active volcanoes in the ocean floor.

"Pyroclastic flows" are deadly, fast-moving currents of gas and volcanic material that can travel downhill at high speeds.

●●●

Magma can take thousands of years to make its way to the surface.

●●●

Diamonds are formed deep within the Earth's mantle, in conditions that can also lead to volcanic activity.

●●●

The last eruption of the Yellowstone supervolcano created a crater nearly 35 miles wide.

●●●

In the Cascade Range of the United States, Mount Rainier (*pictured left*) is considered one of the most dangerous volcanoes due to its large amount of glacial ice.

Some of the oldest rocks on Earth, called "zircons," were formed in magma.

•••

About 80% of the Earth's surface, both above and below sea level, was formed by volcanic activity.

•••

Most of the active volcanoes on Earth are located underwater, along the seafloor.

•••

The smallest volcano in the world is the Taal volcano, located in the Philippines.

•••

Volcanic rocks found on the moon are evidence of its volcanic activity billions of years ago.

•••

The Arenal volcano in Costa Rica (*pictured right*) was dormant for hundreds of years before it suddenly erupted in 1968.

VOLCANO
Quiz

So you think you're a volcano expert now?! Let's find out! Answers are on the following page.

1   What is the difference between magma and lava?

2   Can you name the three main types of volcanoes?

3   How are volcanoes formed?

4   What role do gas and pressure play in volcanic eruptions?

5   What is the Volcanic Explosivity Index (VEI)?

6   What is the 'Ring of Fire', and why is it important in volcanology?

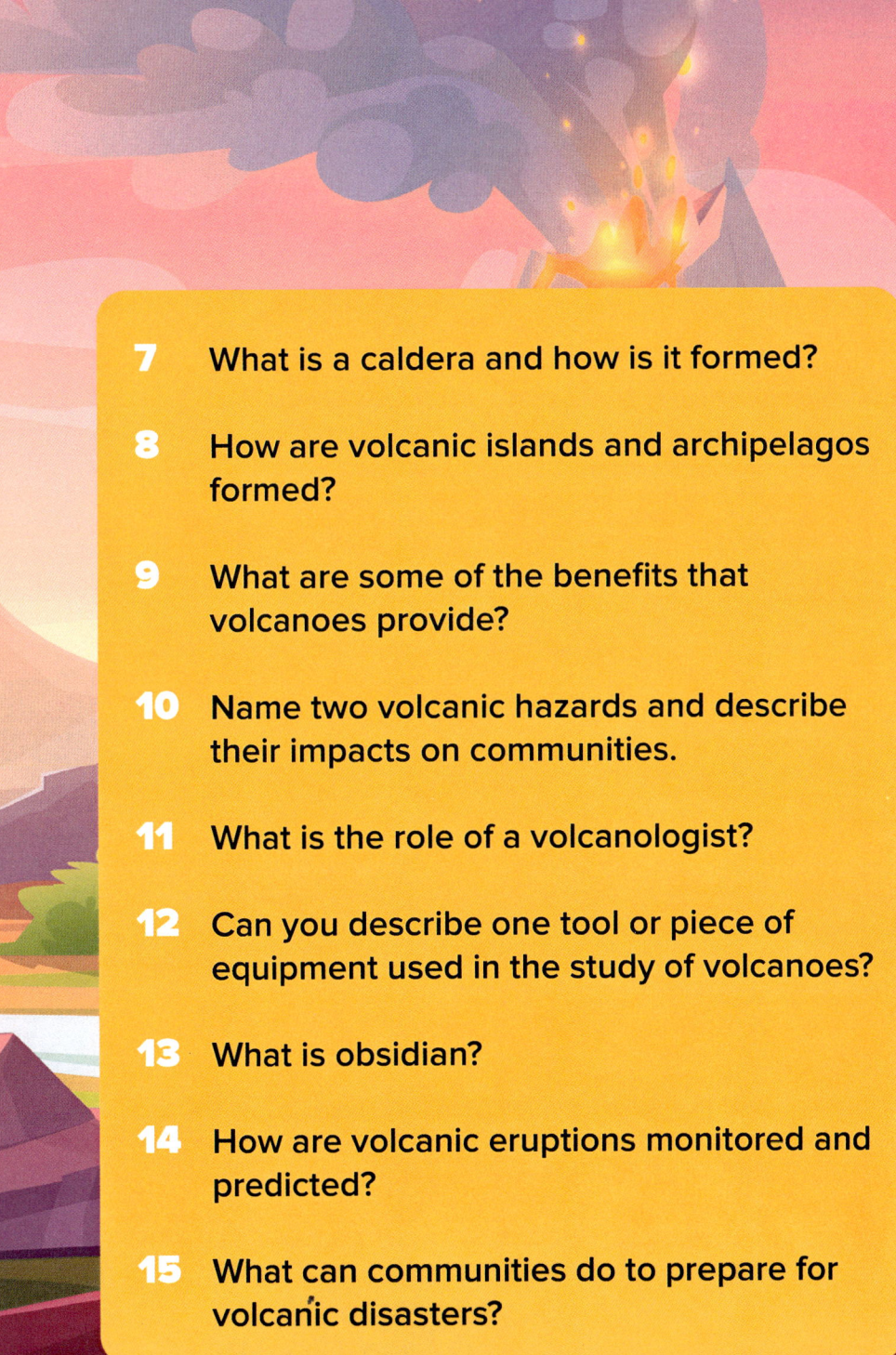

7   What is a caldera and how is it formed?

8   How are volcanic islands and archipelagos formed?

9   What are some of the benefits that volcanoes provide?

10   Name two volcanic hazards and describe their impacts on communities.

11   What is the role of a volcanologist?

12   Can you describe one tool or piece of equipment used in the study of volcanoes?

13   What is obsidian?

14   How are volcanic eruptions monitored and predicted?

15   What can communities do to prepare for volcanic disasters?

Active Rabaul Volcano, Papua New Guinea.

ANSWERS

1. Magma is molten rock beneath the Earth's surface, and lava is molten rock that has erupted onto the Earth's surface.
2. The three main types of volcanoes are shield volcanoes, cinder cone volcanoes, and composite or stratovolcanoes.
3. Volcanoes are formed by the movement of tectonic plates, either where plates are moving apart (divergent boundaries) or coming together (convergent boundaries).
4. Gas and pressure play a critical role in causing the magma to erupt from the volcano. The gas bubbles expand causing pressure to build, and when the pressure is too great, an eruption occurs.
5. The Volcanic Explosivity Index (VEI) is a relative measure of the explosiveness of volcanic eruptions.
6. The 'Ring of Fire' is a major area in the Pacific Ocean where a large number of earthquakes and volcanic eruptions occur due to the boundaries of several tectonic plates.
7. A caldera is a large cauldron-like hollow that forms following the emptying of a magma chamber in a volcanic eruption.
8. Volcanic islands and archipelagos are formed by volcanic activity, often where one tectonic plate is subducting under another.
9. Some benefits of volcanoes include the creation of fertile soil, mineral deposits, geothermal energy, and attracting tourism.
10. Volcanic hazards can include lava flows which can burn and bury structures, ash clouds which can cause respiratory issues and affect aviation, and lahars which can bury towns and change landscapes.

11. A volcanologist is a geologist who specializes in studying volcanoes.
12. Seismometers to measure earthquakes, gas analyzers to measure gas emissions, and thermal cameras to measure heat output are just a few examples.
13. Obsidian is a type of glass formed when lava cools rapidly.
14. Volcanic eruptions are monitored with various geophysical tools to measure seismic activity, gas emissions, and ground deformation. Computer models can help predict eruptions based on this data.
15. Communities can prepare for volcanic disasters by having emergency plans in place, educating the public about what to do in an eruption, and building structures to divert lava flows.
16. Volcanoes impact climate by releasing gases like carbon dioxide that can warm the planet, and particulates that can cool it. Large eruptions can affect the global climate.
17. Hawaii has a chain of volcanoes, including some of the world's most active, and is made entirely of volcanic islands.
18. Diamonds form deep within the Earth's mantle under high temperature and pressure conditions, these areas often also have volcanic activity which brings the diamonds to the surface in a special kind of rock called kimberlite.
19. The smallest volcano in the world is the Taal Volcano, located in the Philippines.
20. Indonesia.
21. Mauna Loa, Hawaii.

WHAT AM I?

Am I a shield volcano, stratovolcano (composite volcano) or a cinder cone volcano?

1

2

3

4

WHERE AM I?

Can you name these famous
volcanoes, and where they are?

Can you find all the words below in the word search puzzle on the right?

MAGMA   PYROCLASTIC   LAVA TUBE

CRATER   SULFUR   TECTONIC

ERUPTION   CALDERA   ICELAND

VOLCANO
WORD SEARCH

```
D C A L D E R A U Y T E
G I U Y T E E C S W G J
F C R A T E R Q Z X C V
D E B V C S U L F U R T
L L T R E S P V C U D E
A A U M V X T Z W D F C
V N H M E R I V C X A T
A D Q D A C O N J H D O
T H F D A G N C B J Y N
U R W V C X M K H F S I
B P Y R O C L A S T I C
E Q K G D A X C V R H J
```

SOLUTIONS

	C	A	L	D	E	R	A				
	I					E					
	C	R	A	T	E	R					
	E				S	U	L	F	U	R	T
L	L				P						E
A	A				T						C
V	N		M		I						T
A	D			A	O						O
T				G	N						N
U					M						I
B	P	Y	R	O	C	L	A	S	T	I	C
E											

What am I?

1. Cinder cone; 2. Stratovolcano; 3. Shield volcano

Where am I?

1. Mount Teide, Canary Islands; 2. Mount St Helens, USA; 3. Mount Fuji, Japan; 4. Mount Etna, Sicily.

SOURCES

"Volcanic Eruptions". 2023. Who.Int. https://www.who.int/health-topics/volcanic-eruptions.

"Smithsonian / USGS Weekly Volcanic Activity Report". 2023. Smithsonian Institution | Global Volcanism Program. https://volcano.si.edu/reports_weekly.cfm.

"Interactive Map Of Volcanoes And Current Volcanic Activity Alerts In The United States". 2015. American Geosciences Institute. https://www.americangeosciences.org/critical-issues/maps/volcano-activity-alerts.

"Shield Volcanoes (U.S. National Park Service)". 2023. Nps.Gov. https://www.nps.gov/articles/000/shield-volcanoes.htm

"Shield Volcanoes". 2010. Volcano World. https://volcano.oregonstate.edu/shield-volcanoes.

Zobin, Vyacheslav M. 2017. "Volcano-Tectonic Earthquakes At Basaltic Volcanoes". Introduction To Volcanic Seismology, 81-118. doi:10.1016/b978-0-444-63631-7.00005-4.

"Ring Of Fire | Definition, Map, & Facts". 2023. Encyclopedia Britannica. https://www.britannica.com/place/Ring-of-Fire.

"Volcano | Definition, Types, & Facts". 2023. Encyclopedia Britannica. https://www.britannica.com/science/volcano.

"17 Explosive Volcano Facts". 2023. https://www.nat-geokids.com/uk/discover/geography/physical-geography/volcano-facts/

"Maunakea Observatories – A Collaboration Of Independent Institutions With Telescopes Located On Maunakea". 2023. Maunakeaobservatories.Org. https://www.maunakeaobservatories.org/.

"Mount St. Helens' 1980 Eruption Still Causing Destruction". 2023. Earthsky | Updates On Your Cosmos And World. https://earthsky.org/earth/this-date-in-science-cataclysmic-eruption-at-mount-st-helens/.

"Information about Volcanologists". USGS. 2023. https://www.usgs.gov/observatories/cascades-volcano-observatory/information-about-volcanologists.

"10 Little-Known Facts About Volcanoes - Earth How". 2019. Earth How. https://earthhow.com/facts-about-volcanoes/.

Wood, C.A. (1979). "Cindercones on Earth, Moon and Mars". Lunar and Planetary Science.

Venzke, E., ed. (2013). "How many active volcanoes are there?". Global Volcanism Program Volcanoes of the World (version 4.9.1). Smithsonian Institution.

GLOSSARY

ACTIVE VOLCANO: A volcano that has had at least one eruption during the last 10,000 years.

ASH: Tiny particles of rock, minerals, and volcanic glass created during a volcanic eruption.

BASALT: A type of igneous rock that makes up most of the ocean floor and many volcanic cones.

CALDERA: A large, bowl-shaped crater formed by an eruption.

CINDER CONE VOLCANO: A type of volcano made mostly of cinders and other rock particles that have been blown into the air.

COMPOSITE OR STRATOVOLCANO: A type of volcano composed of many layers of hardened lava, tephra, and volcanic ash.

CRATER: A bowl-shaped pit at the top of a volcano.

DORMANT VOLCANO: A volcano that has not erupted for a very long time but could erupt again in the future.

ERUPTION: The release of materials from the Earth's crust through an opening or vent.

EXTINCT VOLCANO: A volcano that has not had an eruption for at least 10,000 years and is not expected to have another eruption.

GEOTHERMAL ENERGY: The heat energy that comes from the Earth's interior.

IGNEOUS ROCK: Rock that forms when hot, molten rock (magma or lava) cools and hardens.

LAHAR: A destructive mudflow on the slopes of a volcano.

LAVA: Molten rock that has reached the Earth's surface.

LAVA TUBE: A natural tunnel within a solidified lava flow, originally formed by the flowing lava.

MAGMA: Molten rock beneath the Earth's surface.

MANTLE: The layer of the Earth below the crust and above the core.

PYROCLASTIC FLOW: A fast-moving current of hot gas and volcanic matter that flows along the ground away from a volcano.

RING OF FIRE: An area in the basin of the Pacific Ocean where many earthquakes and volcanic eruptions occur.

SEISMOMETER: An instrument that measures and records details of earthquakes, such as force and duration.

SHIELD VOLCANO: A type of volcano usually built almost entirely of fluid lava flows.

TECTONIC PLATES: Large plates of rock that make up the surface of the Earth, these move, collide and slide past each other, often causing earthquakes and volcanic activity.

VENT: An opening in the Earth's surface where volcanic material erupts.

VOLCANIC EXPLOSIVITY INDEX (VEI): A relative measure of the explosiveness of volcanic eruptions.

VOLCANOLOGIST: A scientist who studies volcanoes and volcanic activity.

VOLCANO: An opening in the Earth's crust through which molten lava, ash, and gases are ejected.

Thanks for joining us on this explosive journey through the world of volcanoes! If you enjoyed this book, please consider leaving a review—they always make us smile!

For more great books, just scan the QR code below, or visit us at:

www.bellanovabooks.com

ALSO BY JENNY KELLETT

  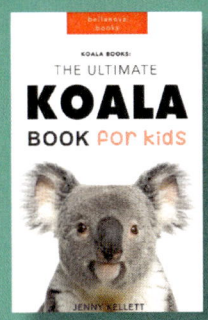

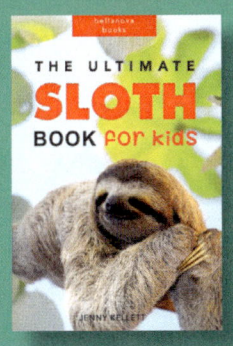 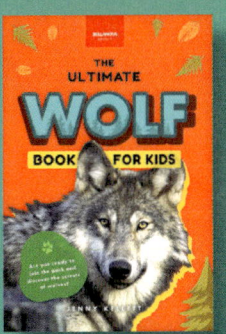 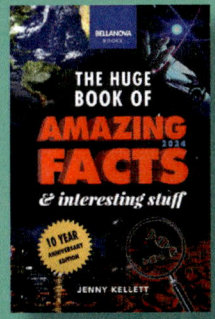

... and more!

Available at

www.bellanovabooks.com

and all major online bookstores.